# TERRA COTTA CUISINE
## RECIPES FOR POTTERY COOKWARE

# Nancy Fair McIntyre
### Illustrations by Maxwell Moray

# Cobble & Mickle Books
# Portland, Oregon

Published by Cobble & Mickle Books, P.O. Box 6533, Portland, Oregon
97228
Cover Design by Margot Thompson, Portland, Oregon, 1990
Printed in the United States of America
You may order single copies of this book direct from the publisher for
$7.95 plus $1.50 postage and handling.
Other Cobble & Mickle cookbook titles:
4 & 20 Blackbirds, Cooking in Crust by Nancy Fair McIntyre
Magnificent Molds, Recipes for Make-Ahead Magic by Nancy Fair
    McIntyre
Great Convertibles, 7 Master Recipes for Superb Dishes from Appetizers
    to Entrees to Desserts by Kit Snedaker
Michael Grant's Cookbook, Hearty Fare From a Country Kitchen by
    Michael Grant
Library of Congress Catalog Card Number 90-82551
ISBN 0-9616524-8-9

# Table of Contents

# *Introduction*

Earthenware cookery is as old as the Romans and as basic as mother earth. It is not only the most versatile of cooking arts, but also the tastiest.

The secret of earthenware cooking is in the clay. Clay has unique properties for cooking any kind of food—as the Romans discovered two thousand years ago. Caesar's banquets served up succulent chickens baked in fresh clay, and savory meats simmered in pottery vessels of *terra cotta,* or "fired clay."

Modern gourmets stir up epicurean delights in a variety of pottery—from earthenware to ceramic. Especially popular with gourmet hostesses are the decoratively shaped cookers and terra cotta roasters that distribute heat so evenly the food requires no basting or turning. These flavorful cookers—some of which are charmingly shaped like chickens, game hens or fish—keep meat, seafood and poultry moist and juicy. Since natural juices are retained—praise Caesar!—there's no shrinkage.

This book features dozens of gala party dishes for these novel cookers and roasters. You'll also find continental recipes for every type of earthenware cookery from simmering soups to sizzling gratins, individual casseroles to communal fondues, practical beans to frivilous souffles. And, of course, we pay special tribute to that classic of them all: the big, mama-sized casserole simmering fragrantly in the oven unmindful of the clock or electronic age.

The slow, gentle simmer that is the secret of the earthenware casserole, makes seasonings sing, flavor intensify, and meat or chicken fork-tender. Earthenware cookery inspires culinary adventures for the imaginative cook who can transform economical cuts of meat into elegant dishes. Humble stews transform into *Boeuf Bourguignonne* or *Navarin of Lamb.*

Since pottery is slow to heat, and retains an even, over all temperature, it is ideally suited for braising and pot roasting—as every canny French housewife knows. The marmite, or large earthenware pot, has been heart and fixture of the Gallic kitchen for centuries. Pottery is the original cook 'n serve ware. It retains heat and travels from oven to table with the greatest of ease.

Recipes in this book are for four people. However, many of the dishes, such as casseroles, are generously figured for second helpings.

Turn the page for helpful tips on caring for your pottery cookware.

Pottery varies from the simple, unglazed, or semi-glazed earthenware to stoneware, or ceramic that is completely glazed.

While some earthenware requires no preparation or "seasoning" before use, most earthenware or *terra cotta,* especially the imported variety, needs initial "seasoning" to render long-lasting service. Usually manufacturers supply directions for using their cookware—which includes instructions on any "seasoning" that is necessary.

One "seasoning" method is to rub the pot inside and out with a clove of garlic, fill it with water, and bake it slowly in a moderate oven for six hours. Another process, recommended particularly for the unglazed terra cotta roasters or cookers, is to pour boiling water over the cooker until completely saturated and then bake it in a 400 degree oven until the cooker is bone dry and all the water has evaporated.

The highly porous, unglazed roasters or cookers require a lining of greaseproof paper, or foil, to prevent loss of juices while cooking. While these unglazed pots afford a unique way of cooking because they're crafted of natural clay, the partially glazed or totally glazed pottery cookers also produce succulent results. So take your pick.

Earthenware should only be cleaned with hot water and a stiff brush. Avoid soap or detergents if possible. Leave pots uncovered and in the fresh air until completely dry before putting them away.

No pottery of any kind should be used on top of the stove without a protective asbestos pad to diffuse the heat.

In most instances, pottery cookware as well as the contents, should be at room temperature before putting it in the oven. When removing, do not place pots directly on a cold or wet surface.

Note: to insure that your domestic or imported earthenware may be safely used, buy it from reputable, experienced manufacturers.

# SOUP CLASSICS

One of the important ingredients in soup is time as well as thyme. The unhurried soup simmers into the most savory brew. The deep earthenware soup pot, or *"marmite"* as it's called in France, retains the heat at just the right temperature to simmer soup gently and flavorfully.

Since this is top-of-the-stove cooking, pots must be protected with an asbestos pad to diffuse the heat.

For easy entertaining, try a soup 'n salad 'n French bread party with one of these classic Gallic potages. A good wine is an important embellishment.

2 lbs chicken, cut into serving pieces
3 Tbsp butter
1 lb brisket of beef
1 lb beef ribs
1 large onion
1 stalk celery (with leaves)
2 qts beef bouillon
1 cup carrots, thinly sliced
1 cup turnips, diced
1/2 cup celery, sliced
1 cup shredded cabbage
salt and pepper to taste

Lightly brown chicken in butter and transfer to a soup pot. Add brisket of beef, beef ribs, onion, celery and bouillon. Simmer for 15 minutes; skim off foam, cover pot, and continue simmering for another 2 hours. Discard onion and celery.

Bone chicken and beef ribs; cut brisket into 1/2 inch squares. Return chicken and meat to pot with carrots, turnips and celery. Cover pot and simmer 1/2 hour; add cabbage and cook 5 minutes more. Season with salt and pepper to taste.

Serve into earthenware soup bowls; and top each bowl with a slice of buttered, toasted French bread.

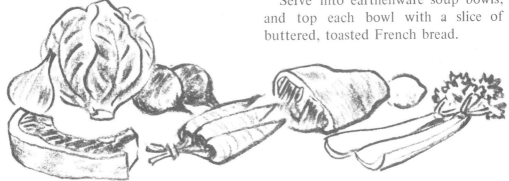

6 red onions, peeled and cut lengthwise
2 Tbsp olive oil
2 Tbsp butter
1 Tbsp sugar
2 qts beef bouillon
1/2 cup dry white wine
salt and pepper to taste
4 slices toasted French bread
4 Tbsp grated Gruyere cheese

Saute onions in a saucepan with olive oil and butter until onions are golden but not browned.

Transfer onions into soup pot and add sugar, beef bouillon, wine, and salt and pepper to taste. Simmer for 1 hour.

Ladle soup into individual earthenware soup bowls, top with toasted French bread and grated Gruyere cheese. Put soup bowls under the broiler until cheese melts and is golden brown.

3 Tbsp olive oil
2 leeks (white part only) thinly sliced
3 cloves garlic, crushed
2 cups tomatoes, peeled and diced
1 carrot, thinly sliced
1 1/2 cups potatoes, diced
1/8 tsp saffron, crumbled
8 cups chicken stock
salt and pepper to taste
4 slices French bread
2 Tbsp olive oil
4 Tbsp grated Parmesan cheese

Heat oil in a skillet and saute leeks and garlic until vegetables are tender. Transfer to a soup pot and add tomatoes, carrot, potatoes, saffron, chicken stock and salt and pepper to taste.

Cover and simmer for 1 hour. Pour soup into earthenware soup bowls.

Brush French bread with olive oil, sprinkle with Parmesan cheese and brown under the broiler. Float a slice of toasted French bread in each bowl of soup before serving.

# *Potage Saint-Germain*

2 cups green split peas
2 qts water
1 stalk celery, thinly sliced
1 carrot, thinly sliced
1 large onion, finely chopped
1 leek (white part only) thinly sliced
1 ham hock
1 1/2 tsp salt
1 tsp pepper
1 bay leaf
4 cups beef bouillon
2 Tbsp butter
1/2 cup heavy cream

Remove bay leaf and discard. Remove ham hock, cut off outside rind, dice meat and add to soup. Puree soup in a blender for a few minutes. Return soup to pot and add beef bouillon, butter, and heavy cream. Briefly reheat and serve from soup pot into earthenware soup bowls.

Wash peas and put into soup pot. Add water, celery, carrot, onion, leek, ham hock, salt, pepper and bay leaf. Cover and simmer for 15 minutes. Skim off foam, cover and continue cooking for 2 1/2 hours or longer, until peas are very soft, and mixture is thick.

4 leeks (white part only) thinly sliced
2 Tbsp butter
3 potatoes, thinly sliced
1/2 cup celery, finely chopped
4 cups chicken stock
salt to taste
1 cup milk, scalded
1 cup half and half
1/2 tsp pepper

Garnish:  croutons and
          chopped parsley

Saute leeks in butter until tender but not browned. Transfer leeks into soup pot and add potatoes, celery, chicken stock and salt to taste. Cover and simmer 30 minutes or until potatoes, celery and leeks are soft.

Pour soup into a blender and puree for a few minutes.

Return soup to pot and stir in milk, half-and-half, and season with pepper. Simmer until hot and serve in earthenware soup bowls. Garnish with croutons and chopped parsley.

# *PARTY FONDUES*

The art of fondue-manship requires flourish, taste—and the right pot.

The classic pottery fondue pot stirs the best cheese fondues. It sits on a rack over an alcohol burner providing just enough heat to melt the cheese and keep the sauce bubbling gently without overheating.

While pottery pots can't be used for fondues requiring hot oil or high temperatures, they're perfect for many chafing dish specialties.

Here's a repertory of cheese fondues that will dazzle your friends. Serve them anytime: as an hors d'oeuvre, first course, late supper or Sunday breakfast.

**1 lb Fontina cheese or Gruyere**
**1 tsp cornstarch**
**1/2 cup milk**
**1/4 tsp salt**
**1/2 tsp white pepper**
**3 egg yolks, beaten**
**2 Tbsp butter, melted**

Cut Fontina or Gruyere cheese into small chunks and place in a fondue pot over alcohol burner.

Dissolve cornstarch in milk and stir into pot. Season with salt and pepper. Slowly heat contents until cheese melts. (Don't worry if cheese is stringy at this point.)

In a bowl, combine egg yolks and stir in melted butter. Gradually add eggs into fonduta and stir until cheese is a light, creamy consistency. Pour fonduta into individual earthenware casseroles and serve with chunks of toasted, buttered Italian bread for dipping.

Fontina cheese may be purchased at gourmet specialty stores or Italian delicatessens.

1 lb Swiss cheese, diced
3 Tbsp flour
1 clove garlic
1 1/4 cups dry white wine
1/4 cup Cognac
Paprika

Sprinkle cheese with flour and mix well.

Rub the inside of fondue pot with garlic. Heat wine in pot over alcohol burner and gradually add cheese, stirring continuously with a wooden spoon until cheese melts. Remove from fire and add warm Cognac.

Sprinkle fondue with a decorative touch of paprika, and serve with bite-size cubes of French bread and fondue forks.

1 lb very sharp Cheddar cheese, diced
1 1/2 tsp dry English mustard
1 Tbsp Worcestershire sauce
Dash of Tabasco sauce
1/4 tsp paprika
1/2 tsp salt
1/4 tsp cayenne pepper
1/2 cup heavy cream

Put cheese in a fondue pot and stir over alcohol burner until cheese melts. Add mustard, Worcestershire sauce, Tabasco, paprika, salt and cayenne pepper. Stir and pour in cream.

Simmer until hot and bubbly and pour over buttered, toasted English muffins. This may be topped with crumbled cooked bacon if you like.

1 envelope onion soup mix
1 12-oz bottle beer
1/2 lb grated Cheddar cheese
1/2 lb grated Swiss cheese
2 Tbsp flour

Combine onion soup mix and beer in fondue pot and heat over alcohol burner.

In a bowl mix together cheddar cheese, Swiss cheese, and flour.

When beer begins to simmer, slowly add combined cheeses gradually, stirring continuously until cheese melts. Keep fondue hot over a small flame.

Serve with French bread cut into bite size cubes, or finger-size slices. Provide small paper plates and fondue forks for the guests to help themselves.

1 cup bread crumbs
1 cup milk
1 Tbsp butter
1 lb Cheddar cheese, diced
1 egg, beaten
1/2 tsp salt
1/4 tsp ground black pepper

Soak bread crumbs in milk for 10 or 15 minutes.

Melt butter in a fondue pot over the alcohol burner. Add cheese and stir until cheese melts. Add soaked breadcrumbs and gradually stir in egg, salt and pepper. Stir until fondue is hot. Spoon out over buttered toast.

# *Fondue Piemonte*

1 lb Fontina cheese, diced
1/2 lb ricotta cheese
1 cup dry white wine
1/4 tsp ground black pepper
1/2 tsp salt
1 egg yolk, beaten
1 whole white truffle, thinly sliced

Combine Fontina and ricotta cheese in fondue pot, and simmer over alcohol burner until cheeses melt. Stir continuously with a wooden spoon. Add wine, black pepper and salt; and simmer until hot.

Remove from fire and gradually stir in egg yolk. Sprinkle with shavings of truffle.

Serve with fondue forks and French or Italian bread cut into large cubes or finger-size slices.

The truffle, Fontina and ricotta cheeses can be purchased at Italian grocery stores, or gourmet specialty shops.

1  10 1/2 oz can tomato soup,
   undiluted
1  lb Cheddar cheese, diced
2  egg yolks, beaten
1 1/2 tsp Worcestershire sauce
1  tsp dry mustard
2  egg whites
1/8 tsp salt

Combine tomato soup and cheese in a fondue pot and heat over an alcohol burner until cheese melts and rarebit is smooth. Stir in beaten egg yolks, Worcestershire sauce and dry mustard. Whip egg whites until stiff and fold into rarebit. Season with salt.

Serve over hot, buttered toast or English muffins.

1 clove garlic
1 1/2 cups dry white wine
3/4 lb Gruyere cheese, grated
3 tsp cornstarch
3 Tbsp Kirschwasser
Freshly ground pepper

Rub the bottom and sides of fondue pot with garlic. Add wine and heat over alcohol burner almost to the boiling point. Add cheese and stir continuously with a wooden spoon until cheese is melted and creamy.

Combine cornstarch with Kirschwasser and stir into fondue. Add pepper and stir until mixture bubbles. Keep fondue hot over a very low flame.

Provide guests with fondue forks and a platter of bite-size cubes of French bread for dipping into the fondue.

If the cheese gets too thick, stir in a little more white wine.

# Cheese Fondue According To Brillat-Savarin

"Weigh the number of eggs which you want to use. This number depends on how many people are going to eat with you.

"Take a piece of good Gruyere weighing a third and butter weighing a sixth of the weight of the eggs.

"Break the eggs and beat them well in a bowl. Add the butter and the cheese, grated or minced.

"Pour mixture into a fondue pot and slowly cook over an alcohol burner, stirring with a wooden spoon, until mixture has suitably thickened and is smooth. Add a very little or hardly any salt, depending on the age of the cheese. Add a good portion of pepper, which is one of the distinguishing characteristics of this dish.

"Serve over triangles of bread sauteed in butter."

# Scotch Rarebit

2 Tbsp butter
1/4 cup green onions, chopped
1/4 cup green pepper, chopped
1/2 lb ground round beef
1/3 cup ale or beer
1/2 tsp salt
1/2 tsp powdered mustard
1/2 tsp paprika
1 Tbsp Worcestershire sauce
1/4 tsp cayenne pepper
3/4 lb Cheddar cheese, diced
4 English muffins,
   cut in halves and toasted

Melt butter in a skillet and saute onions and green pepper for several minutes. Add meat and crumble with a fork; stir until brown.

Heat ale or beer in a fondue pot over alcohol burner. Add salt, powdered mustard, paprika, Worcestershire sauce and cayenne pepper. Add cheese and stir over low heat until cheese is melted.

Drain meat and vegetables from skillet and stir into rarebit. Briefly heat. Serve over English muffins.

# *FESTIVE FOWL*

Earthenware or ceramic, these decorative chicken cookers are conversation pieces that cook. They can be used for all kinds of meats or casseroles; and, for roasting fowl they're inspired. (The following recipes recommend pre-browning before roasting which gives a richer color to poultry and meat.)

We might also note that while basting is not needed to keep food moist, it enhances the over-all flavor when you're cooking with savory sauces or wine.

The main course of a dinner party deserves festive presentation and a little immodest fanfare; so bear your pottery bird to the table with all due ceremony!

# Poulet Bonne Femme

1/4 lb lean salt pork, diced
4 Tbsp butter
8 small white boiling onions, peeled
2 carrots, thinly sliced
1 leek (white part only) thinly sliced
4 to 5 lb roasting chicken
1 cup dry white wine
1 tsp salt
1/4 tsp pepper
1/2 tsp rosemary
1/2 tsp thyme
1 clove garlic, crushed

Saute salt pork in a skillet until crisp and lightly browned. Remove pork, melt butter and saute onions, carrots and leek until vegetables are tender and golden brown. Remove vegetables and brown chicken in the same skillet.

Truss chicken and place in cooker. Spoon vegetables and diced pork around fowl and pour over white wine. Season chicken with salt, pepper, rosemary, thyme and garlic. Cover and roast in a preheated 400 degree over for 2 hours, or until chicken is tender.

Serve chicken with vegetables and diced pork. This dish goes well with cooked artichoke hearts and sauteed cap mushrooms.

2 Tbsp butter
2 Tbsp olive oil
4 to 5 lb roasting chicken
1 tsp salt
1/2 tsp pepper
1/2 tsp tarragon
3 Tbsp brandy
3 Tbsp butter
1 green pepper, seeded and diced
1 sweet red pepper, seeded
　and diced
1 tomato, peeled, seeded
　and diced
3 Tbsp cooked ham, diced
4 green onions, thinly sliced
1 clove garlic, minced
1/2 tsp salt
1/4 tsp pepper

Heat butter and olive oil in a skillet and lightly brown chicken on all sides. Season with salt, pepper and tarragon.

Truss chicken and place in a chicken cooker. Pour remaining butter and olive oil in skillet over chicken. Cover, and roast in a preheated 400 degree oven for 2 hours, or until chicken is tender.

Pour warm brandy over chicken, ignite; when flame dies out, cover cooker and keep chicken warm.

Melt butter in a saucepan and saute green pepper, red pepper, tomato, ham, onions and garlic until vegetables are soft and tender. Season with salt and pepper. This *Basquaise* sauce should be spooned over the chicken just before serving.

4 Tbsp butter
4 Rock Cornish game hens
2 tsp salt
4 tsp grated orange rind
3 Tbsp lime juice
1 tsp Worcestershire sauce
1 Tbsp Cointreau
6 Tbsp orange marmalade
2 Tbsp brandy

Melt butter in a skillet and lightly brown game hens. Season bird cavities with salt. Place birds in individual foil-lined game hen cookers or two chicken cookers. Pour remaining butter in skillet over birds.

In a bowl combine grated orange rind, lime juice, Worcestershire sauce, Cointreau, orange marmalade and brandy. Blend well and let sauce stand 1 hour to blend flavors. Spoon mixture equally over game hens.

Cover and roast in a preheated 400 degree oven for 45 minutes to 1 hour, or until birds are tender.

In recipes such as this, where a sauce has a sweet ingredient, it is best to line your cooker with foil paper—even if the pot is glazed inside. When sugar encrusts the bottom of a pan, it is difficult to clean.

4 Tbsp butter
4 to 5 lb roasting chicken
1 onion, finely chopped
1/4 cup celery, finely chopped
2 Tbsp parsley, chopped
1 1/2 cups tomato juice
1 chicken bouillon cube
1/2 tsp salt
1/4 tsp pepper
1/2 tsp rosemary
6 green olives, pitted and sliced
6 black olives, pitted and sliced

Melt butter in a skillet and lightly brown chicken on all sides. Remove chicken and saute onion, celery and parsley in remaining butter for 5 minutes. Add tomato juice and chicken bouillon cube and stir until hot.

Truss chicken and place in chicken cooker. Pour over tomato sauce. Season chicken with salt, pepper and rosemary. Cover and roast in a preheated 400 degree oven for 2 hours, or until chicken is tender.

Remove chicken from cooker, strain juices, skim off fat, and add green and black olives to sauce. Simmer for 2 or 3 minutes. Return chicken to cooker, and pour sauce over chicken before serving.

4 Tbsp butter
2 tsp dry mustard
4 to 5 lb roasting chicken
1 tsp salt
1/2 tsp pepper
2 Tbsp butter
1/3 cup dry bread crumbs
1 Tbsp parsley, chopped

Garnish: chopped crisp bacon

Melt butter in a skillet and stir in mustard. Lightly brown chicken in mustard butter. Truss chicken and put into cooker. Pour over remaining mustard-butter and season with salt and pepper. Cover and roast in a 400 degree oven for 1 1/2 hours.

Melt butter in a skillet and saute bread crumbs until golden brown. Sprinkle breadcrumbs and parsley over chicken, and continue roasting for 1/2 hour, or longer, until bird is tender.

Top with chopped crisp bacon before serving.

5 Tbsp butter
4 to 5 lb Beltsville midget turkey
1 tsp salt
1 tsp thyme
1/2 tsp basil
1/4 cup butter
1/2 cup skinless roasted peanuts,
    finely chopped
1 1/2 cups dry breadcrumbs
1 onion, finely chopped
1/2 cup cornbread, crumbled
1/2 cup hot chicken broth
1 egg, beaten
salt and pepper to taste
1/4 cup white wine
1/4 cup brandy

Melt butter in a skillet and lightly brown turkey on all sides. Season cavity and skin with salt, thyme and basil. Place turkey in cooker and pour over remaining butter.

Melt another 1/4 cup of butter in a separate skillet and brown peanuts.

In a bowl combine peanuts, melted butter, bread crumbs, onion, cornbread, hot chicken broth and beaten egg. Salt and pepper to taste. Mix well and stuff turkey cavity. Fasten opening with skewers and truss bird. Place turkey in chicken cooker, cover, and roast in a preheated 400 degree oven for 1 hour.

Pour white wine and brandy over turkey, cover; continue roasting for another 1 1/2 hours, or until turkey is tender. Leave turkey in cooker 1/2 hour after removing from oven before carving.

Since turkey tends to be the driest of all poultry, we suggest regular basting. The result will be the most moist and succulent turkey you've ever eaten.

3 Tbsp butter
4 to 5 lb roasting chicken
3 shallots, peeled and finely chopped
1/2 cup white wine
1/2 cup chicken broth
1 bay leaf
1/2 tsp thyme
1 Tbsp parsley, chopped
1 tsp tarragon
1 tsp salt
1/4 tsp pepper
2 Tbsp lemon juice
1/2 cup heavy cream
2 Tbsp flour

Melt butter in a skillet and lightly brown chicken on all sides. Remove chicken and saute shallots in butter until golden brown. Add white wine, chicken broth, bay leaf, thyme, parsley and tarragon. Simmer for 3 or 4 minutes.

Truss chicken and place in cooker. Pour over wine-broth sauce. Season with salt and pepper. Cover cooker and roast in a preheated 400 degree oven for 1 hour. Squeeze lemon juice over chicken and continue roasting for 1 hour, or until bird is tender.

Remove chicken and strain juices. Combine juices and heavy cream in a skillet and stir in flour mixed with 1 Tbsp of water. Simmer until sauce thickens.

Return chicken to cooker; pour sauce over it and garnish with fresh tarragon leaves before serving.

6 4( . 6 3( C77

6 4( . 33 B 88 b

br
pla

gre
is tender. During cooking pour off all
excess fat.

Melt butter in a second skillet and
aute shallots for 5 minutes. Add wine
ind chicken broth. Drain cherries re-
erving 1/2 cup of cherry juice. Mix
herry juice with cornstarch and stir
nto skillet. Season sauce with salt and
epper and simmer until it slightly
hickens. Add drained cherries and simmer another 5 minutes. Pour over duck
before serving.

## Chapter IV

These picturesque fish cookers cook and serve the best seafood in the world—and that's no fish story. Like the chicken cookers, they retain the natural moisture of foods. This is especially important with fish that tends to dry out during cooking.

These old world style cookers, which come in various sizes, are available in earthenware or ceramic; and are an enchanting image of the delicacy they bring to the table. They inspire seafood dishes to delight the eye as well as the pallette.

Use them for whole baked fish, or fish steaks—as well as your favorite seafood casseroles. In fact, these versatile cookers cook anything—even hot dogs. They're not proud.

3 Tbsp butter
2 Tbsp green onions, minced
1 packaged frozen chopped
   spinach, thawed
1 1/2 cups soft white breadcrumbs
4 Tbsp heavy cream
1 Tbsp lemon juice
1/2 tsp salt
1/4 tsp paprika
1/4 tsp pepper
4 lb whole fish (or section of fish)
   cleaned and boned
1 cup dry vermouth
3 Tbsp butter

Melt butter in a saucepan and saute onions 1 minute. Squeeze water from thawed spinach and add to onions, stirring another minute.

In a bowl combine onion-spinach mixture with breadcrumbs, heavy cream, lemon juice, salt, paprika and pepper. Stuff fish cavity with this mixture and close opening with toothpicks, or skewers, and lace with string.

Place fish in the bottom of a buttered fish cooker. Pour vermouth over fish and dot with butter. Cover and bake in a preheated 350 degree oven for 45 minutes to 1 hour, or until fish flakes easily with a fork. Serve this succulent seafood with hollandaise sauce.

1 lb shrimp
1/3 cup onion, finely chopped
1 rib celery, finely chopped
1/2 clove garlic, minced
2 Tbsp olive oil
1 cup white wine

2 cups water
1/2 tsp salt
2 Tbsp onion, finely chopped
4 Tbsp butter
1 cup white rice
1/3 cup Parmesan cheese, grated

Shell and devein shrimp, reserving shells.

Saute onion, celery and garlic in olive oil until vegetables are lightly cooked. Add shrimp and stir a few minutes longer.

In a separate saucepan, combine shrimp shells, wine, water and salt. Cover pan and simmer 10 minutes. Strain stock and skim.

In another skillet, melt butter and add rice—stirring until rice is golden.

Combine rice, vegetables, and shrimp in a fish cooker. Pour 2 cups of hot shrimp stock over mixture. Cover and bake in a 350 degree oven for 30 minutes, or until rice is tender, and liquid has been absorbed. Sprinkle with Parmesan cheese 5 minutes before taking casserole from oven.

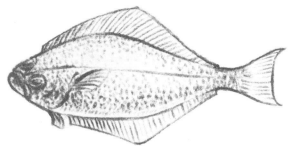

4 Tbsp butter
1 carrot, finely chopped
1 small onion, finely chopped
2 shallots, finely chopped
1/4 lb mushrooms, finely chopped
2 Tbsp celery, finely chopped
1 Tbsp parsley, finely chopped
1/2 tsp thyme
4 Tbsp ham, finely diced
1/2 tsp salt
1/4 tsp pepper
4 halibut steaks
3/4 cup white wine
3 Tbsp butter
1/4 tsp paprika
2 Tbsp lemon juice

Melt butter in a skillet and add carrot, onion, shallots, mushrooms, celery, parsley, thyme and ham. Season with salt and pepper and saute until vegetables are soft.

Spread half the vegetable-ham mixture in the bottom of a buttered fish cooker and place the halibut steaks on top. Spread steaks with the remaining vegetable-ham mixture and pour white wine over-all. Dot fish with butter and season with paprika. Cover and bake in a preheated 350 degree oven for 20 minutes, or until fish flakes easily with a fork. Squeeze lemon juice over dish before serving.

1  4-lb snapper, cleaned and boned
1 cup white wine
1/2 tsp salt
1/2 tsp pepper
1/4 cup butter
1 cup mushrooms, sliced
6 green onions, thinly sliced
2 cups cooked wild rice
1/2 cup cream-of-mushroom soup,
    undiluted
1 egg, beaten
1/4 tsp salt
4 Tbsp butter

Sprinkle snapper with 3 Tbsp of wine. Rub salt and pepper into fish cavity.

Melt butter in a saucepan and saute mushrooms and onions until tender. Combine vegetables with the cooked wild rice, cream of mushroom soup, egg and salt.

Stuff snapper loosely with this dressing and close the cavity with wooden toothpicks or skewers and lace with string to contain the dressing.

Place the fish in a buttered fish cooker, dot with butter, and add remaining wine. Cover and bake in a preheated 350 degree oven for 45 minutes to one hour, or until fish flakes easily with a fork.

2 Tbsp butter
1 cup mushrooms, finely chopped
1 1/2 cups cooked shrimp, shelled,
    deveined and finely chopped
1 egg, beaten
1 cup heavy cream
1/4 cup white wine
1/2 tsp salt
1/4 tsp pepper
4 lb whole fish (or section of fish)
    cleaned and boned

Melt butter in a skillet and saute mushrooms for 1 minute.

In a bowl, combine mushrooms with shrimp, egg, 1/2 cup of cream and white wine. Season with salt and pepper.

Stuff fish cavity with shrimp-mushroom mixture and close cavity with wooden toothpicks, or skewers, and lace with string.

Place fish in a buttered fish cooker. Pour over remaining 1/2 cup of cream, cover and bake in a preheated 350 degree oven for 45 minutes to 1 hour, or until fish flakes easily with a fork.

1 package curry-flavored rice
4 Tbsp butter
1/4 cup celery, finely chopped
1/2 cup green onions, finely chopped
1 green pepper, finely chopped
1/4 lb fresh mushrooms, sliced
7 1/2-oz can cooked crabmeat, boned and flaked

1 lb cooked shrimp, shelled and deveined
2 Tbsp pimiento, chopped
1/2 tsp Accent
2 tsp curry powder
2 10 1/2-oz cans cream-of-mushroom soup, undiluted
1/4 cup slivered almonds, toasted

Cook rice according to directions on package.

Melt butter in a skillet and saute celery, onions, pepper and mushrooms until vegetables are tender. Combine vegetables with cooked rice, crabmeat, shrimp, pimiento, Accent and curry powder. Stir in mushroom soup and blend well.

Pour into buttered fish cooker. Sprinkle with toasted almonds. Cover and bake 15 or 20 minutes in a preheated 350 degree oven.

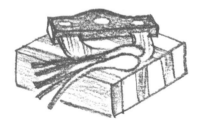

4 salmon steaks
2 Tbsp butter, melted
4 Tbsp butter
1/2 lb mushrooms, finely chopped
1/2 lb cooked shrimp, peeled,
    deveined and finely chopped
1/2 tsp salt
1/2 pint sour cream

Brush salmon steaks with melted butter.

Melt additional butter in a saucepan and saute mushrooms until tender. Add shrimp and simmer a few minutes. Spread mushroom-shrimp mixture over the salmon steaks, season with salt and place in a buttered fish cooker. Spoon sour cream over fish. Cover and bake in a preheated 350 degree oven for 20 minutes, or until fish flakes easily.

1 1/2 cups shelled oysters
1 1/2 cups oyster liquor
8 slices bacon, cut in 1-inch lengths
1 onion, finely chopped
3 cups canned Italian plum tomatoes
1 tsp salt
1/4 tsp pepper
2 Tbsp pimiento, finely chopped
1 cup rice
1 1/2 cups cooked shrimp, shelled
    and deveined

Simmer oysters in oyster liquor for 5 minutes. (If you do not have sufficient oyster liquor to make 1 1/2 cups, water may be added to liquor). Reserve liquor.

In a skillet fry bacon until crisp; remove bacon and saute onion in bacon fat until onion is tender but not brown. Mash tomatoes with a fork and add to skillet with oyster liquor, salt, pepper, and pimiento. Simmer 3 minutes. Pour tomato sauce into the top of a double boiler, and add rice. Steam rice until it is cooked in about 1/2 hour. Add a little water if more liquid is needed.

Pour rice and tomato sauce into a buttered fish cooker and stir in the oysters, bacon and cooked shrimp. Bake in a preheated 350 degree oven for 15 minutes.

# COOKING IN CLAY

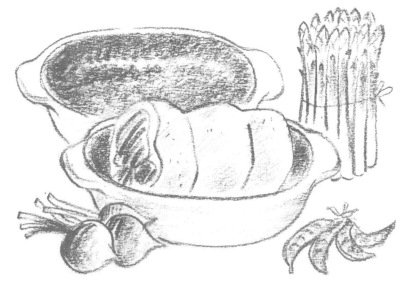

These terra cotta roasters are another classic innovation of earthenware cooking. Derived from ancient Roman cookers, their way with meat is legendary. They roast or braise meat to delectable, juicy tenderness and work the same magic on poultry or seafood.

3 lb center-cut loin of pork
1 clove garlic, crushed
1 tsp salt
1 tsp allspice or cinnamon
1/4 tsp pepper
1 cup cooked prunes, pitted
2 Tbsp butter
1 cup dry white wine
8 small white boiling onions, peeled

Have butcher saw off outside chine bone and cut three-quarters of the way through the pork between the bones to make pockets for stuffing.

Mix garlic, salt, allspice or cinnamon and pepper. Rub mixture over meat and into pockets. Fill each pocket with three prunes. Tie roast together with a string to keep compact and prevent stuffing from coming out.

Quickly brown pork in butter. Place meat in roaster and pour over white wine. Cover and roast in a 400 degree oven for 1 1/2 hours. Add onions and continue cooking for another 1/2 hour, or until pork is tender.

4 lb leg of lamb, boned
2-oz can anchovy fillets
pine nuts
2 Tbsp butter
2 Tbsp olive oil
1 clove garlic, crushed
1 tsp salt
1/2 tsp rosemary
1/2 tsp pepper
1 cup red wine

Lay anchovy fillets in the cavity of the boned lamb and roll and tie roast with a string. Make 6 or 8 incisions in the lamb with a small knife and insert pine nuts.

Brown lamb in hot butter and olive oil. Rub lamp with garlic, salt, rosemary and pepper. Put lamb in a roaster and pour in red wine.

Roast in a preheated 400 degree oven for 2 hours or longer, depending on how pink or well done you prefer your lamb.

3 lb rolled rump veal roast
2 Tbsp butter
1 tsp salt
1/2 tsp pepper
1/2 tsp rosemary
3 strips lean salt pork
1/2 cup beef consomme
1/2 cup dry white wine
2 Tbsp flour
1/4 cup water

Garnish: chopped parsley

Quickly brown veal in butter. Season veal with salt, pepper and rosemary. Lard roast with strips of salt pork. Place veal in roaster and pour consomme and white wine over veal. Roast in a pre-heated 400 degree oven for 2 hours, or until veal is tender.

Pour off juices into skillet and skim off fat. Mix flour and water and stir into gravy. Simmer a few minutes until gravy thickens.

Remove salt pork from roast, and slice. Spoon over gravy. Serve with an accompanying vegetable platter of potato balls, string beans and broiled tomatoes, dressed in butter and garnished with chopped parsley.

3 lb center cut pork loin
3 Tbsp butter
1 clove garlic
1 tsp salt
1 tsp sage
1/2 tsp peppercorns
1/2 tsp nutmeg
1 onion, thinly sliced
2 carrots, thinly sliced
1/2 cup Vermouth
1/2 cup water
1/2 cup red current jelly
2 tsp dry mustard
5 or 6 whole cloves

Quickly brown meat in butter.

With a mortar and pestle, mash together garlic, salt, sage, peppercorns, and nutmeg. Rub mixture over pork loin.

Spread onions and carrots on the bottom of foil-lined roaster and place meat on top. Pour vermouth and water over meat. Cover and roast in a pre-heated 400 degree oven for 1 hour.

Remove meat and slash top of roast in a crisscross diamond pattern such as that used on baked ham. Combine current jelly with dry mustard. Spread glaze over meat and stud with cloves.

Continue roasting at 400 degrees for 1 1/4 hours, or until pork is tender.

# Roast Beef Teriyaki

2 cups beef bouillon
2/3 cup Japanese soy sauce
1/2 cup red wine
1/4 cup green onions, finely chopped
3 Tbsp brown sugar
2 Tbsp lemon juice
2 tsp powdered ginger
2 cloves garlic, crushed
3 lb rolled rib roast of beef

In a large bowl combine beef bouillon, soy sauce, red wine, green onions, brown sugar, lemon juice, ginger and garlic. Place rolled rib roast in marinade and marinate meat in the refrigerator at least 5 or 6 hours. Turn meat occasionally.

Drain meat and reserve marinade. Place beef in a foil-lined roaster. (Even if your roaster is glazed inside, in this instance it's important to use foil. The sugar in the marinade tends to burn the bottom of the pan during cooking.)

Cover roaster and roast meat in a preheated 400 degree oven, allowing 32 minutes per lb for rare beef and 40 minutes per lb for medium well done. A meat thermometer is advisable to insure the exact degree of pinkness you desire. Baste frequently with marinade during cooking.

Leave roast in roaster 20 minutes after removing from oven to let the juices settle.

Strain marinade, heat and serve separately with roast.

# CONTINENTAL CASSEROLES

This plump earthenware casserole has survived progress and electronic cookery to remain the first, and best of the casseroles. It has given birth to more of the world's great dishes than any other cooking pot. On the following pages you'll find classic, old world special-ties—many of which originated in the earthenware casserole.

3 cups white beans
2 qts water
1/2 lb bacon rind
1/2 lb slab bacon (in one piece)
3 cloves garlic, minced
1 tsp thyme
1 1/2 Tbsp salt
1/2 tsp pepper
1/2 tsp basil
1/2 tsp marjoram
1 lb fresh sausage
1 lb pork, cut into 1 1/2 inch chunks
1 cooked roasted chicken, cut in
   small serving pieces
1 cup dry breadcrumbs
3 Tbsp butter, melted
1/4 cup parsley, finely chopped

Wash beans and put in large pot. Add water and bring to a boil. Boil 2 minutes, remove from heat and let beans soak 1 hour. Add bacon rind, bacon, garlic, thyme, salt, pepper, basil and marjoram. Cover and simmer slowly for 1 1/2 hours, or until beans are tender.

Meanwhile, grill sausage in a skillet until brown. Remove and quickly brown chunks of pork.

Remove bacon rind from beans and discard. Cut the slab bacon into 3/4 inch squares. Spoon out 1/3 of the beans into a large casserole. (Cassoulet is traditionally baked in an earthenware casserole). Over the top of the beans place pieces of roasted chicken. (Rotisserie-roasted chicken available in delicatessens and markets may be used if you don't want to roast your own chicken.) Cover chicken with another layer of beans and add pork, grilled sausage, and bacon. Pour over the rest of the beans and bean juices, which should be plentiful. If there isn't enough liquid to almost cover the beans, add some canned chicken stock.

Sprinkle with breadcrumbs and melted butter, cover and bake for 4 hours or longer, in a preheated oven at 250 degrees. The last 1/2 hour remove cover to give the Cassoulet a rich brown crust. Sprinkle with parsley just before serving.

Cassoulet should be juicy so don't forget to add more chicken broth, or water, to casserole during baking if necessary.

1 lb 11-oz can sauerkraut
1/2 lb lean bacon
1 onion, finely chopped
3 carrots, thinly sliced
1 large tart apple, peeled,
   cored and sliced
1 tsp cracked peppercorns
1/2 tsp salt
6 juniper berries, or 2 Tbsp gin
4 slices smoked ham,
   1/4-inch thick
3 Tbsp butter
1 cup chicken stock
1 cup white wine
1 lb smoked Polish sausage

Rinse sauerkraut in cold running water and drain well.

Line casserole with bacon slices. Place a layer of sauerkraut over bacon and cover with a layer of onions, carrots and apples, using half the quantity of each. Sprinkle with peppercorns, salt and juniper berries or gin. Top with a layer of smoked ham slices. Add another layer of vegetables and finish with a layer of sauerkraut. Dot with butter and pour chicken stock combined with white wine over casserole.

Cover and bake in a preheated 250 degree oven for 4 hours. Add more wine or chicken stock if needed. The last 40 minutes of baking, add Polish sausage to casserole.

Serve with whole, peeled boiled potatoes dusted with chopped parsley.

3 lb corned beef
1 tsp salt
6 peppercorns
1 onion studded with 3 cloves
1/4 cup brown sugar
4 medium-sized potatoes, quartered
4 carrots, quartered
4 turnips, quartered
1/2 lb smoked Polish sausage
1 small cabbage head

Garnish: parsley sprigs

Place corned beef in casserole and cover with cold water. Add salt, peppercorns, onion and brown sugar. Bring casserole to a boil on top of the stove (over an asbestos pad) and skim off foam.

Transfer covered casserole to pre-heated, 300 degree oven and simmer for 4 hours or until meat is tender. The last 1/2 hour add potatoes, carrots, turnips and sausage. The last 10 minutes add cabbage.

Slice meat and arrange on a large platter with sliced sausage and vegetables. Garnish with parsley sprigs and serve with condiments of cream-horseradish and mustard.

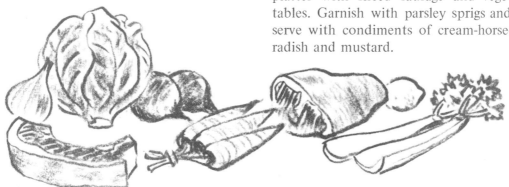

2 small chickens (2 to 3 lbs)
   cut in serving pieces
Juice of 2 lemons
2 tsp salt
1/2 tsp pepper
1/4 cup olive oil
1/4 lb cooked ham, diced
6 green onions, chopped
4 tomatoes, peeled and quartered
1 green pepper, seeded and chopped
1 sweet red pepper, seeded and
   chopped
1 Tbsp parsley, chopped
1 bay leaf
1/4 tsp saffron
3 cups boiling chicken broth
1 1/2 cups white rice
1/4 cup sherry wine

Garnish: Sauteed mushroom caps

Brush chickens with lemon juice and sprinkle with salt and pepper. Heat olive oil in a skillet and quickly brown chicken; transfer to a casserole.

Saute ham in the skillet until lightly browned and add green onions, tomatoes, green pepper, red pepper, parsley, bay leaf and saffron. Simmer 5 or 6 minutes. Pour mixture over chicken. Add chicken broth, cover and bake in a 325 degree oven for 1 hour.

Add rice and stir. Continue baking another 1/2 hour or until rice is cooked and has absorbed most of the juices. The last 5 minutes of cooking, stir in sherry. Garnish with sauteed mushroom caps.

# Navarin Of Lamb

2 lbs lean boneless lamb,
  cut in 1-inch chunks
1/2 cup flour
3 Tbsp olive oil
2 cloves garlic, minced
1/2 cup white wine
1 cup tomato puree
2 cups beef bouillon
1/2 tsp thyme
1 tsp salt
1/2 tsp pepper
8 small white boiling onions, peeled
3 carrots, quartered
2 turnips, quartered
1 package frozen peas, thawed

Dust lamb in flour. Heat olive oil in a skillet and brown garlic. Add lamb and lightly brown. Put lamb and garlic in a casserole.

Pour off excess fat in skillet and add wine, tomato puree, beef bouillon, thyme, salt and pepper. Bring to a simmer and pour over meat.

Cover casserole and bake in a preheated 300 degree oven for 1 1/2 hours. Add onions, carrots, turnips, and more liquid if necessary; and continue baking another 1/2 hour. The last 10 minutes, stir in peas.

1 large bacon rind
3 lb eye-of-the-round beef
1 clove garlic, crushed
1 tsp salt
1 tsp pepper
1/4 tsp nutmeg
1/4 tsp cinnamon
3 whole cloves
3 Tbsp bacon, diced

1 onion, quartered
3 carrots, cut in 3-inch strips
3 shallots, peeled and sliced
2 bay leaves
sprig of parsley
1 tsp rosemary
2 cups Burgundy wine
1/4 cup brandy
1 cup beef bouillon

Place bacon rind in the bottom of a casserole.

Rub meat with crushed garlic, salt, pepper, nutmeg and cinnamon. Lay meat on bacon rind and add cloves, diced bacon, onion, carrots, shallots, bay leaves, parsley and rosemary. Pour in Burgundy wine, brandy and beef bouillon. Liquid should almost cover meat, if not add more beef bouillon.

Cover top of casserole with heavy foil before replacing the lid. Bake at 350 degrees for 1 hour. Reduce heat to 250 and slowly simmer for 4 more hours, or until meat is tender. Remove bacon rind before serving.

# Braised Oxtails

2 lbs oxtails, disjointed
1/2 cup flour
1/2 tsp salt
1/2 tsp pepper
4 Tbsp butter
1 onion, finely chopped
2 carrots, chopped
1 leek (white part only) thinly sliced
2 ribs of celery, chopped
1 clove garlic, minced
2 Tbsp parsley, chopped
1 bay leaf
1 tsp rosemary
1/2 tsp thyme
1/2 tsp salt
2 cups canned Italian plum tomatoes
8 small white boiling onions
1/4 tsp powdered cloves
1 cup beef bouillon
1 cup Burgundy wine
1 cup sliced fresh mushrooms

Wash and dry oxtails. Dredge in flour, and season with salt and pepper.

Melt butter in a saucepan and quickly brown oxtails. Remove from pan and add onion, carrots, leek, celery and garlic. Saute vegetables until tender and lightly browned.

Transfer oxtails and vegetables to a casserole and season with parsley, bay leaf, rosemary, thyme and salt. Add tomatoes, onions, cloves, beef bouillon and wine. Liquid should almost cover contents, if insufficient, add additional wine and beef stock.

Cover and bake in a preheated 300 degree oven for 2 hours. Add mushrooms and continue baking another 1/2 hour.

# Boeuf Bourguignonne

2 lbs chuck beef, cut
   into 1 1/2-inch chunks
1/2 cup flour
3 Tbsp butter
3 Tbsp olive oil
1/2 tsp salt
1/2 tsp pepper
4 Tbsp warm Cognac
1/4 lb bacon, diced
1 clove garlic, minced
1 carrot, thinly sliced
1 leek (white part only) thinly sliced
1 onion, chopped
1 bay leaf
1/2 tsp thyme
1 Tbsp parsley, chopped
2 cups Burgundy wine
1 Tbsp butter
1 Tbsp flour
2 Tbsp butter
12 small boiling onions, peeled
 8 mushroom caps


Dredge beef in flour.

In a saucepan heat butter and olive oil and quickly brown meat. Season with salt and pepper. Pour warm Cognac over meat and ignite. When flame dies out, transfer meat to a casserole.

In the same saucepan, saute bacon, garlic, carrot, leek and onion until bacon is slightly crisp and vegetables are tender.

Add contents to casserole with bay leaf, thyme and parsley. Pour in burgundy wine with sufficient water to barely cover meat. Cover and bake in a preheated 300 degree oven for 2 hours.

Blend butter and flour together and gradually stir into casserole. Cover and continue baking another 2 hours until the meat is fork tender.

Meanwhile, melt butter in a skillet and saute onions until lightly browned. Remove and saute mushroom caps a few minutes. Add onions to casserole the last 1/2 hour. Garnish Boeuf Bourguignonne with mushrooms just before serving.

4 small carrots, peeled and quartered
10 small white boiling onions, peeled
1/2 lb green beans, cut
      into 2-inch lengths
1 qt chicken stock
1/2 lb fresh green peas, shelled

4 whole potatoes, peeled
1/2 tsp salt
1/4 tsp pepper
1 tsp basil
3 Tbsp butter, melted
1 Tbsp parsley, chopped

Put carrots, onions and green beans in a saucepan and pour chicken stock over them. Cover and simmer for 8 minutes.

Transfer vegetables and liquid to a casserole. Add fresh peas, potatoes, salt, pepper and basil. Cover casserole and simmer in a preheated 325 degree oven for 45 minutes.

Pour out all but 1 cup of chicken stock. Spoon melted butter over vegetables, sprinkle with parsley, and serve from casserole.

This ragout may be varied by adding asparagus, zucchini, turnips, or other vegetables.

2 cups dried lima beans
2 qts water
3 lbs brisket of beef
2 onions, chopped
4 Tbsp butter
2 tsp salt
1/2 tsp pepper
1/2 tsp ginger
1 cup pearl barley
2 Tbsp flour
2 tsp paprika
1 tsp salt

Put lima beans in a saucepan with water, bring to a boil and cook for 2 minutes. Remove from fire and let beans soak 1 hour.

Brown brisket of beef and onions in butter, and sprinkle with salt, pepper and ginger. Place meat and onions in a casserole and cover with drained lima beans and barley, then sprinkle with flour, paprika and salt. Add sufficient hot water to cover contents 1 inch.

Cover and bake in a preheated 300 degree oven for 4 to 5 hours. During cooking, check casserole to see if more water should be added to keep Cholent moist.

Slice meat and serve with the lima beans and barley.

2 packages frozen spinach, thawed
1 lb ricotta cheese
3 eggs, lightly beaten
2/3 cup grated Parmesan cheese
1/3 cup parsley, chopped
2 tsp salt
1/2 tsp pepper
1/4 cup olive oil
1 1/2 cups onion, finely chopped
1 carrot, finely chopped
2 cloves garlic, minced
4 cups canned Italian plum tomatoes
1/2 tsp salt
1/2 tsp pepper
4 Tbsp butter
1 tsp oregano
1 tsp basil
1 lb elbow macaroni
    (medium-sized)
 2 Tbsp salt

Cook spinach according to directions on package. Press out all the water from the spinach and combine it with the ricotta cheese, eggs, Parmesan cheese, parsley, salt and pepper.

Make a Marinara sauce by heating olive oil in a saucepan into which onions, carrot and garlic are sauteed until lightly browned. Add tomatoes, salt and pepper and simmer 15 minutes; mash tomatoes with a fork into a sauce consistency. Add butter, oregano and basil. Combine Marinara sauce with the ricotta-spinach mixture.

Meanwhile cook macaroni in 6 qts boiling salted water for only 2 minutes. Drain in a colander and pour macaroni into a casserole.

Stir in Marinara sauce, cover and bake 25 to 30 minutes in a 350 degree oven until macaroni is tender but not mushy. Serve with additional Parmesan cheese.

# Coq Dijon

2 small chickens (2 to 3 lbs),
 cut in serving pieces
2 tsp salt
1/2 tsp pepper
1/2 tsp paprika
1/2 tsp nutmeg
1 cup flour
4 Tbsp butter
1/4 lb bacon, diced
8 small white boiling onions, peeled
1 clove garlic
1 cup mushrooms, sliced
1/2 tsp tarragon
1/2 tsp rosemary
1 bay leaf
1 Tbsp parsley, chopped
3 oz brandy
3 cups Burgundy wine

Season chickens with salt, pepper, paprika and nutmeg. Dip chickens in flour lightly.

In a saucepan melt butter and add bacon, stirring until bacon is lightly browned. Remove bacon and quickly brown chickens. Remove chicken and saute onions and garlic in saucepan until golden brown. Add mushrooms and stir 2 minutes.

Transfer vegetables, chicken and bacon to casserole. Season with tarragon, rosemary, bay leaf and parsley. Pour brandy over chicken and ignite. When the flame burns out, pour in Burgundy wine. Cover and bake in a preheated 300 degree oven for 2 hours.

If necessary, add a little more wine, or water, during cooking.

3 lbs boneless lamb, cut
  in 1 1/2 inch chunks
2 Tbsp butter
2 Tbsp olive oil
1 large onion, chopped
1 clove garlic, minced
1 tsp salt
2 cups consomme
1 onion, sliced
1/2 lb string beans, cut
  in 2-inch lengths
1 green pepper, seeded and sliced
2 small zucchini, sliced
1 eggplant, peeled and cubed
1  10-oz package frozen baby okra,
  thawed
2 large tomatoes, cut in wedges
3 Tbsp parsley, chopped
1/2 tsp salt
1/2 tsp pepper
1/2 tsp basil
1/2 tsp oregano
1 tsp lemon juice

Brown lamb in hot butter and olive oil. Add onion and garlic and saute until golden brown. Transfer contents to a casserole, season with salt and pour in consomme.

Cover and bake in a preheated 300 degree oven for 1 1/4 hours. Add onion, string beans, green pepper, zucchini, eggplant, okra, tomatoes and parsley. Season with salt, pepper, basil, oregano and lemon juice. Add additional water if necessary.

Cover and continue cooking for another 40 minutes, or until vegetables are cooked.

1/4 lb bacon, diced
1 3-lb bottom round of beef
1 clove garlic, minced
1 onion, chopped
2 carrots, chopped
1 leek (white part only) sliced
1 tsp salt
1/2 tsp coarse ground pepper
3 sprigs parsley
1 bay leaf
1 tsp thyme
1 1/2 cups water
1 cup red wine
3 cups consomme
6 Tbsp tomato paste
1 Tbsp cornstarch
2 Tbsp water
1 3-oz jar black pitted olives
2 Tbsp butter
12 cherry tomatoes

Cook bacon in a skillet until lightly browned. Remove bacon and quickly brown beef in bacon fat. Remove meat and saute garlic, onion, carrots and leek until tender.

Transfer vegetables together with beef and bacon into a casserole. Season with salt, pepper, parsley, bay leaf and thyme. Pour in water, wine, consomme and tomato paste.

Cover and simmer in a preheated 300 degree oven for 2 1/2 to 3 hours. Remove meat and keep warm.

Strain stock and skim off fat. Boil stock in a saucepan until it is reduced to 2 cups. Combine cornstarch with 2 Tbsp of water and add to hot stock gradually, stirring constantly. Add black olives to sauce.

Melt butter in a skillet and saute cherry tomatoes until hot.

Slice beef and garnish with sauteed tomatoes. Serve sauce separately.

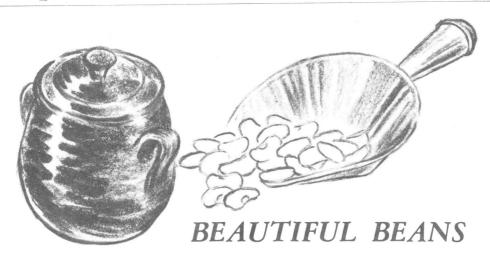

# *BEAUTIFUL BEANS*

The bean pot is a cherished friend of the family from Boston to Burgundy. Nothing is more satisfying or economical than the versatile bean. Sweet, hot, plain or fancy, beans are always welcome; and when homemade, they rate as party food.

The bean from Boston is great; but do try this lovable legume, continental-style in red wine—or flavored with cream and Parmesan cheese. Or, for a change, bake up some Bavarian lentils in your New England bean pot!

2 cups white beans (Great Northern)
2 qts water
1 Tbsp salt
1 bay leaf
1 stalk celery with leaves
1 sprig parsley
3/4 lb lean salt pork
1 onion, finely chopped
1/3 cup molasses
1/4 cup brown sugar
1 Tbsp dry mustard
1/4 tsp pepper
1/2 cup sherry wine

Put beans in a saucepan with water and bring to a boil. Boil beans for 2 minutes, remove from stove and soak for 1 hour. Add salt, bay leaf, celery, parsley, and simmer until beans are barely tender in about 1 hour. Drain beans, discard celery, bay leaf, parsley, and reserve liquid.

Cut salt pork into pieces 1 inch square and 1/4 inch thick. Put beans, salt pork and onion in alternate layers in a bean pot, reserving a few pork slices for the top.

Combine molasses, brown sugar, mustard, and pepper with sufficient bean liquid to cover beans. If necessary, supplement bean liquid with hot water.

Lay pork slices over the top, cover pot and bake in a slow, 250 degree oven for 4 to 5 hours. Pour sherry over beans the last hour of baking.

Make certain there is sufficient liquid to cover beans when they're baking; and add water or bean liquid if necessary. If you like crusty beans, leave the cover off the bean pot the last 1/2 hour of baking.

2 cups white beans (Great Northern)
2 qts water
6 cups chicken broth
salt to taste
1/2 cup onions, chopped
1/3 cup carrots, diced
3 Tbsp butter
1/2 cup heavy cream
2 Tbsp parsley, chopped
2 Tbsp butter
2 Tbsp flour
1 cup milk
1/2 tsp salt
2 Tbsp grated Parmesan cheese

Put beans in a saucepan with water. Bring to a boil and cook 2 minutes. Remove from stove and soak 1 hour. Drain beans and add chicken broth. Season with salt to taste. Simmer 1 1/2 hours or until beans are tender.

Saute onions and carrots in butter until vegetables are tender. Combine vegetables with drained beans and stir in heavy cream. Add chopped parsley.

Melt butter in a skillet, stir in flour and gradually add milk stirring until sauce thickens. Season with salt.

Combine this white sauce with beans and vegetables and transfer to a bean pot. Top with Parmesan cheese, cover and bake for 45 minutes in a 300 degree oven.

3 cups canned red kidney beans
1/3 cup onions, finely chopped
1 Tbsp butter
1/4 lb bacon, diced
2 Tbsp flour
1 cup red wine
1/2 tsp salt
1/4 tsp pepper

Drain beans.

Saute onions in butter until tender. Add bacon and cook until bacon is browned but not crisp. Drain off all but 2 Tbsp fat. Sprinkle bacon-onion mixture with flour and stir. Pour in wine and cook until sauce thickens. Season with salt and pepper.

Combine with beans and pour into a bean pot. Cover and bake in a 300 degree oven for 20 minutes.

2 cups dried lentils (quick cooking)
1 onion, studded with 3 cloves
1 bay leaf
1 Tbsp salt
1 Tbsp parsley, chopped
4 knockwurst, quartered lengthwise
2 Tbsp butter
3 strips bacon

Wash lentils and put them in a large saucepan with water to cover. Add onion, bay leaf and salt. Simmer for 30 minutes. Drain lentils and reserve liquid. Discard onion and bay leaf. Sprinkle lentils with parsley.

Saute knockwurst in butter until nicely browned.

Spoon 1/3 of the lentils into a bean pot and top with a layer of knockwurst. Add another layer of lentils and knockwurst and a final topping of lentils. Pour lentil liquid over top.

Cook bacon until crisp. Crumble bacon over lentils, cover bean pot and bake for 40 minutes in a 350 degree oven.

# Continental Bean Pot

2 cups white beans (Great Northern)
2 qts water
1 bay leaf
1 onion studded with 2 cloves
1 Tbsp salt
1/2 tsp pepper
1 clove garlic
1 cup cooked ham, cut into
  small chunks
1/2 cup tomato puree
1/2 cup beef bouillon
2 Tbsp breadcrumbs
2 Tbsp grated Parmesan cheese

Put beans in a large saucepan with water and bring to a boil. Cook beans for 2 minutes, remove from stove and soak 1 hour. Add bay leaf, onion, salt, pepper and garlic. Cover and simmer until beans are tender in about 1 1/2 hours. Drain beans reserving liquid, and discard onion, garlic and bay leaf.

Combine beans with ham chunks and put into a bean pot.

Mix tomato puree with beef bouillon and sufficient bean stock to cover beans. Cover and bake for 50 minutes in a 350 degree oven. Remove cover and sprinkle top with breadcrumbs and Parmesan cheese. Continue baking another 15 minutes or until top is brown and crusty.

# AU GRATIN

What is a gratin? Technically, it's a dish sprinkled with breadcrumbs and melted butter, then browned under the broiler or in the oven. Cheese may, or may not, be added. Gastronically speaking, gratin is a touch of genius, the final topping to a beautiful dish that makes it golden brown, sizzling and slightly crusty.

"Au gratin," (French for "in the gratin style"), glamourizes vegetables, enlivens fish dishes, and embellishes almost anything. Gratins can be baked in any shallow earthenware dish; or, if you're a purist, a traditional gratin dish.

1 1/2 lb cooked brisket of beef,
  or pot roast, sliced
2 large sweet white onions,
  thinly sliced
3 Tbsp butter
1 onion, thinly sliced
2 Tbsp butter
2 Tbsp flour
1 cup consomme
1/2 cup, white wine
1/3 cup dry breadcrumbs
2 Tbsp butter
chopped parsley

Remove any fat from cooked beef.

In a skillet saute onions in butter until soft and golden. Line a buttered shallow dish with 1/4 of the onions and place a layer of beef slices on top. Repeat layers of onions and meat, finishing with the beef.

In another skillet, melt butter and saute another thinly sliced onion until it's soft. Sprinkle with flour and blend well. Stir in consomme and white wine. Simmer a few minutes until sauce begins to thicken.

Pour over casserole, top with breadcrumbs, and dot with butter. Bake in a 375 degree oven for 20 minutes. Garnish with parsley before serving.

4 whole bunches endive
2 Tbsp butter
1/2 tsp salt
1/2 tsp sugar
1 tsp lemon juice
1 cup boiling water
4 slices boiled ham
3 Tbsp butter
3 Tbsp flour
1 1/4 cups half-and-half
  (milk and cream)
1/4 cup grated Swiss cheese
1/4 cup white wine
1/2 tsp salt
3 Tbsp grated Parmesan cheese
2 Tbsp dry breadcrumbs
2 Tbsp butter

Wash endive in cold water without tearing leaves apart. Place endive in saucepan and dot with butter. Season with salt, sugar and lemon juice. Pour in boiling water, cover and gently braise endive for 1/2 hour.

Remove endive from saucepan; wrap ham slices around each bunch and fasten with a wooden tooth pick. Arrange endive in a buttered shallow dish.

Melt butter in a skillet and stir in flour. Gradually add half-and-half, grated Swiss cheese and white wine. Season with salt. Stir until cheese melts and sauce thickens. Pour sauce over endive and sprinkle with Parmesan cheese and breadcrumbs. Dot with butter and bake in a 400 degree oven for 10 minutes or until breadcrumbs and cheese are golden brown.

3 Tbsp butter
1 onion, thinly sliced
1 1/2 cups white rice
3 cups chicken stock, boiling
2 cups cooked chicken, diced
3 Tbsp butter
3 Tbsp flour
1/2 tsp salt
1/4 tsp pepper
3/4 cup heavy cream
3/4 cup milk
6 Tbsp grated Swiss cheese
3 Tbsp dry breadcrumbs
2 Tbsp butter

Melt butter in a saucepan and saute onion until transparent. Add rice and stir until rice is coated with butter and golden. Add chicken stock, cover and cook about 15 minutes until rice has absorbed liquid.

Spoon rice into a buttered shallow dish making a ring of the rice. Fill center of ring with the cooked chicken.

Melt butter in a skillet and stir in flour. Simmer 1 minute without browning. Season with salt and pepper and gradually stir in heavy cream and milk, stirring constantly until sauce is smooth and creamy. Add 3 Tbsp of Swiss cheese and stir until cheese melts. Pour sauce over rice and chicken, then sprinkle with the remaining Swiss cheese. Top with breadcrumbs, dot with butter. Brown in 350 degree oven until top is golden brown.

2 Tbsp butter
3 Tbsp onion, finely chopped
2 lbs ripe tomatoes, seeded,
   peeled and chopped
1 tsp salt
1/4 tsp pepper
3 Tbsp heavy cream
1 tsp flour
3 Tbsp butter
2 small eggplants, peeled
1/2 tsp salt
1/4 tsp pepper
1/2 cup flour
4 Tbsp butter
1/2 cup grated Swiss cheese
1/4 cup dry breadcrumbs
2 Tbsp butter

Melt butter in a saucepan and saute onion until golden. Add tomatoes, salt and pepper and simmer for 10 or 15 minutes until tomatoes are soft.

In a separate sauce pan combine heavy cream, flour, and butter. Stir over low flame 1 minute, and add to the tomato mixture.

Cut eggplants in lengthwise slices 1/4-inch thick and season with salt and pepper. Dip slices in flour and saute in butter until tender. Place a layer of eggplant in the bottom of a buttered shallow dish and top with a layer of the tomato-onion sauce. Sprinkle with Swiss cheese. Add another layer of eggplant over which pour the remaining sauce. Top with remaining Swiss cheese. Sprinkle with breadcrumbs and dot with butter.

Brown in a 450 degree oven until the cheese is brown and bubbly.

# *Sole au Gratin*

2 Tbsp butter
2 shallots, peeled and finely chopped
1 Tbsp parsley, chopped
1 tsp chives, chopped
1/2 lb fresh mushrooms,
   finely chopped
1 Tbsp flour

1/2 cup breadcrumbs
4 filets of sole
1/2 tsp salt
1/4 tsp pepper
3/4 cup white wine
3 Tbsp grated Parmesan cheese
3 Tbsp butter

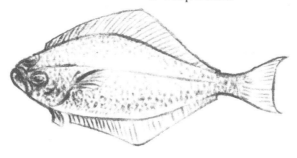

Melt butter in a skillet and saute shallots, parsley, chives and mushrooms for 2 minutes.

Spread half of this mixture in the bottom of a buttered shallow dish which has been dusted with flour. Sprinkle 1/4 cup of the breadcrumbs over the mushrooms. Place sole filets in dish and season with salt and pepper. Cover with the remaining mushroom mixture, and pour in white wine. Sprinkle with the remaining 1/4 cup of breadcrumbs and Parmesan cheese. Dot with butter and bake in a 350 degree oven for 15 to 20 minutes until the top of the dish is delicately browned.

# Stuffed Baked Mushrooms 77

2 lb large fresh mushrooms
3 oz blue cheese, crumbled
4 Tbsp butter
1 cup dry breadcrumbs
1 Tbsp chives, minced
1/4 cup sherry wine
1/2 cup heavy cream

Wash and dry mushrooms; remove stems. Place a small piece of blue cheese in each cavity.

Melt butter in a skillet and saute breadcrumbs until they're coated in butter and golden brown. Mix crumbs and chives with remaining blue cheese. Spoon a layer of this mixture on the bottom of a buttered shallow dish.

Lay the mushrooms, cavity side up, on top of the crumbs. Dribble wine on top. Sprinkle with the remaining breadcrumb mixture and pour cream over all. Bake in a 350 degree oven for 20 minutes.

This mushroom specialty makes an original and savory accompaniment to steak or roast beef.

12 large shrimp
1/2 tsp salt
1/4 tsp pepper
3 Tbsp butter
1/2 cup green onions, chopped
1/2 cup mushrooms, finely chopped
1 clove garlic, minced
1/2 tsp tarragon
1 hard-cooked egg, finely chopped
1/2 cup heavy cream
salt and pepper to taste
1 cup soft breadcrumbs
1 egg yolk, beaten
2 Tbsp parsley, chopped
4 Tbsp grated Parmesan cheese
4 Tbsp butter, melted

Garnish: paprika

Peel shells off shrimp but leave the tails intact. Clean and devein shrimp. With a knife split the underside of the shrimp lengthwise but do not cut all the way through. Spread apart and flatten or "butterfly" the almost divided halves of the shrimp with the flat edge of a heavy knife. Place shrimp in a buttered shallow dish and season with salt and pepper.

Melt butter in a skillet and saute green onions and mushrooms for 3 minutes. Add garlic and tarragon and simmer 1 minute longer. Add chopped egg, heavy cream, and salt and pepper to taste and simmer until hot. Remove skillet from fire and stir in breadcrumbs, egg yolk, and parsley. Spoon this mixture on each shrimp in equal amounts. Sprinkle with Parmesan cheese and pour melted butter over shrimp.

Place under broiler and cook about 8 to 10 minutes until shrimp are golden brown. Garnish with paprika.

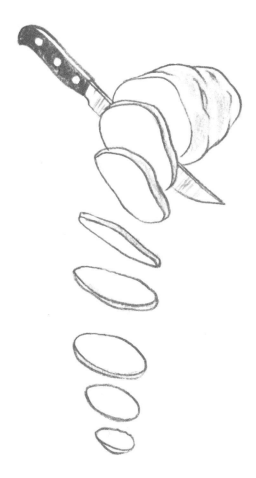

4 medium sized potatoes,
  peeled and thinly sliced
2 cups milk
1 tsp salt
1/4 tsp pepper
1/2 cup heavy cream
1/4 tsp nutmeg
1/4 cup Parmesan cheese
3 Tbsp breadcrumbs
2 Tbsp butter
1/2 tsp paprika

Cook potatoes in milk in the top of a double boiler for 30 minutes. Season with salt and pepper.

Transfer contents to buttered shallow dish and pour heavy cream over potatoes. Season with nutmeg. Sprinkle with Parmesan cheese and breadcrumbs. Dot with butter.

Bake in a moderate oven (350 degrees) for 20 minutes. Top with paprika just before serving.

1/2 box lasagne
1 package frozen chopped spinach,
  thawed
2 Tbsp butter
1/2 lb ricotta cheese
1/4 tsp nutmeg
1/4 tsp marjoram
2 Tbsp grated Parmesan cheese
salt and pepper to taste
2 eggs, beaten
4 Tbsp butter
4 Tbsp flour
2 cups milk
4 Tbsp grated Parmesan cheese
1/2 tsp salt
1/4 tsp cayenne
3 Tbsp dry breadcrumbs
3 Tbsp butter

Cook lasagne according to directions on box. Flush with cold water, and drain. Cut each strip in half crosswise.

Cook thawed spinach 3 minutes and press out all water; stir in butter until melted. Mix spinach with ricotta cheese, nutmeg, marjoram, Parmesan cheese and salt and pepper to taste. Stir in eggs and mix well.

Place the squares of lasagne on a flat surface. Cover the top of each square with a heaping spoonful of the spinach-ricotta mixture. Roll squares up "jelly roll fashion" and lay the stuffed pasta squares in a buttered shallow dish with the fold facing downwards.

Melt butter in a skillet and stir in flour. Simmer 1 minute without browning. Gradually add milk, stirring constantly until white sauce is smooth and creamy. Season with Parmesan cheese, salt and cayenne pepper. Pour sauce over cannelloni and top with breadcrumbs. Dot with butter. Brown in a very hot oven (425 degrees) for 10 to 15 minutes.

2 packages of frozen cauliflower
2 Tbsp butter
2 Tbsp flour
1/4 cup heavy cream
3/4 cup chicken stock
4 Tbsp grated Parmesan cheese
4 Tbsp Swiss cheese
1/2 tsp salt
1/4 tsp pepper
3 Tbsp dry bread crumbs
2 Tbsp butter

Cook cauliflower according to directions on package. Drain.

Melt butter in a saucepan and add flour. Stir and cook 1 minute without browning. Gradually stir in heavy cream and chicken stock and continue cooking until sauce is smooth and creamy. Add 2 Tbsp of Parmesan cheese and 2 Tbsp of Swiss cheese and salt and pepper. Simmer sauce 1 minute.

Pour a little sauce in the bottom of a buttered shallow dish before placing the cooked cauliflower in it. Pour remaining sauce over cauliflower, sprinkle with remaining cheese and breadcrumbs, then dot with butter. Bake in a 400 degree oven until golden brown.

## NEST EGGS

Individual casseroles serve up personal feasts from oven to table. These *"cocottes,"* as they are called in French, bake a variety of tempting dishes from hot hors d'oeuvres to entrees and desserts. They're particularly great for luncheon specialties such as shirred eggs.

Party eggs are dressed for fun with bright seasonings, and festive garnishes. Combined with various foods, baked eggs make a sophisticated entree.

Here are several tasty ways of glamourizing the good egg.

4 thin slices ham
4 thin slices Swiss cheese
1 green pepper, seeded and diced
2 tomatoes, peeled, seeded and diced
2 Tbsp butter
4 eggs
1/2 cup heavy cream
4 Tbsp butter, melted
salt and pepper to taste
1/2 tsp paprika

Line four buttered individual casseroles with 1 slice ham and 1 slice Swiss cheese.

Saute green pepper and tomatoes in butter until vegetables are soft. Spoon out vegetables equally around the sides of the 4 casserole dishes and place dishes in a shallow pan of hot water over low flame.

Break 1 egg in the middle of each dish. Cover with 2 or 3 Tbsp cream and 1 Tbsp butter. Season with salt, pepper and paprika. Simmer eggs for 2 or 3 minutes in hot, but not boiling, water.

Remove; cover casseroles with foil; and bake in a preheated 325 degree oven for another 8 minutes, or until egg whites are firm and yolk is soft.

8 hard-cooked eggs, peeled
1  16-oz can asparagus tips
4 Tbsp butter
4 Tbsp flour
2 cups half-and-half
   (milk and cream)
1 tsp salt
1/4 tsp paprika
1/2 cup dry breadcrumbs
3 Tbsp butter

Cut eggs in thin slices.
Drain asparagus tips and cut in half.

In a skillet melt butter and stir in flour. Gradually stir in half-and-half and cook until cream sauce is thick and creamy. Season with salt and paprika.

Place a layer of egg slices in the bottom of 4 buttered individual casseroles and top with a layer of asparagus tips. Spoon out a little cream sauce over top. Repeat layers ending with cream sauce. Sprinkle breadcrumbs on top of casseroles and dot with butter. Place casseroles under the broiler until breadcrumbs are golden brown.

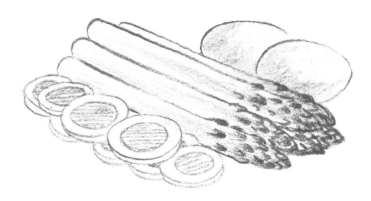

2 medium-sized cooked potatoes,
    thinly sliced
1 small onion, finely chopped
4 Tbsp butter
2 large tomatoes, peeled and diced
4 Tbsp canned small peas, drained
4 eggs
1 tsp salt
1/2 tsp pepper
1 cooked "chorizo" (Mexican sausage),
    skinned and cut in 1-inch lengths
            — or —
4 cooked link sausages, cut in half

Garnish: canned asparagus tips
                and pimiento strips

Saute potatoes and onions in butter until golden.

In another skillet simmer tomatoes for 5 or 6 minutes until soft. Put potatoes and onions in the bottom of 4 buttered, individual casseroles and top with cooked tomatoes. Sprinkle peas around the edges of each dish.

Place casseroles in a shallow pan of hot water over a low flame. Break 1 egg into the center of each casserole. Season casseroles with salt and pepper. Surround eggs with slices of cooked chorizos, or cooked link sausages. Simmer casseroles in pan of water for 2 or 3 minutes.

Remove casseroles, cover with foil and bake in a preheated 325 degree oven for 8 minutes, or until whites of eggs are firm. Garnish with asparagus tips and pimiento strips.

1 1/2 cups cooked chicken,
   finely ground
1/4 cup sauteed mushrooms,
   finely chopped
1/3 cup canned white sauce
4 eggs

1 tsp salt
1/4 tsp pepper
4 Tbsp heavy cream
4 tsp butter, melted
1/2 tsp paprika
2 Tbsp parsley, chopped

Combine chicken with sauteed mushrooms and white sauce. Line 4 buttered individual casseroles with chicken-mushroom mixture.

Place dishes in a shallow pan of hot water over a low flame.

Break 1 egg into each dish, and season with salt and pepper. Cover egg with 1 Tbsp heavy cream, 1 tsp butter and garnish with paprika and chopped parsley. Simmer egg in pan for 2 or 3 minutes.

Remove casseroles, cover with foil paper and bake in a preheated 325 degree oven for another 8 minutes, or until whites of eggs are firm.

1 package frozen spinach, thawed
2 Tbsp butter
4 eggs
1 tsp salt
1/4 tsp pepper
4 Tbsp heavy cream
4 Tbsp Parmesan cheese

Cook spinach for 3 or 4 minutes and drain well, pressing out all water. Add butter to spinach and stir until melted. Line the bottom and sides of 4 buttered individual casserole dishes with spinach.

Put dishes in a shallow pan of hot water over a low flame.

Make an indentation in the center of the spinach and break 1 egg into the hollow. Season with salt and pepper. Spoon out 1 Tbsp of warm heavy cream over each egg and sprinkle with 1 Tbsp of Parmesan cheese. Simmer in pan of water 2 or 3 minutes.

Remove casseroles, cover with foil and place in a preheated 325 degree oven. Bake for 8 minutes until whites of eggs are firm.

# STATUS SOUFFLES

Who would imagine that the airy, celestial souffle could be made in a down-to-earth earthenware dish? These straight-sided earthenware casseroles, glazed inside, render the most beautiful and billowing souffles this side of Paris.

Souffles rise to any social occasion. Looking and tasting wickedly extravagant, they advertise your well-traveled tastes. If the evening calls for image-building or a few status symbols, bring on the souffle for dessert. Remember, however, that souffles are as temperamental as divas and must be served when ready. So time your dinner accordingly.

To test whether a souffle is done, insert a knife in its center. Knife should come out clean.

2 Tbsp butter
3 Tbsp flour
3/4 cup milk
1 lemon rind, grated
1 orange rind, grated
4 Tbsp orange marmalade
1/4 tsp salt
2 Tbsp sugar
3 egg yolks, beaten
1/2 tsp salt
5 egg whites
1/2 cup pecan nuts, grated
1 Tbsp sugar
1/2 cup sour cream
1 Tbsp grated lemon rind
1 Tbsp sugar

**Garnish: powdered sugar**

Melt butter in the top of a double boiler and add flour. Stir in milk and cook until sauce thickens. Add grated lemon rind, orange rind, marmalade, salt and sugar. Beat 2 or 3 Tbsp of hot sauce into the egg yolks and gradually stir eggs back into sauce. Remove from stove, and stir this custard until it cools.

Add salt to egg whites and beat whites until stiff. Fold into orange-lemon custard.

Sprinkle bottom of buttered 1 1/2 qt souffle dish with pecans and sugar and pour in souffle. Bake in a pre-heated 375 degree oven for 30 to 35 minutes. Garnish with powdered sugar.

Serve with an accompanying sauce of sour cream flavored with grated lemon rind and sweetened with sugar.

2 oz unsweetened chocolate
3 Tbsp butter
1/4 cup flour
1 cup milk, hot
5 Tbsp sugar
3 egg yolks, beaten
2 tsp vanilla
2 Tbsp rum
1/4 tsp salt
1/4 tsp cream of tartar
1 Tbsp sugar
3 egg whites

Garnish: whipped cream

Melt chocolate in the top of a double boiler. Add butter and stir until blended.

Stir a little of the hot chocolate into the flour and stir flour back into the chocolate; then cook for 1 minute to form a roux, or thick mixture of butter, flour and chocolate. Gradually stir in hot milk and sugar, and continue stirring until sauce thickens. Remove from stove and beat chocolate sauce for 1 minute and slowly add egg yolks, vanilla and rum.

Combine salt, cream of tartar and 1 Tbsp sugar with egg whites and beat whites until they are stiff. Fold egg whites into chocolate sauce and pour into a 1 qt souffle dish.

Bake in a preheated 375 degree oven for 25 to 30 minutes. Garnish with whipped cream.

3 Tbsp butter
3 Tbsp flour
1/3 cup heavy cream
3/4 cup coffee
4 egg yolks, beaten
1/2 cup sugar
1/4 cup blanched, toasted,
    ground almonds
3/4 tsp vanilla
5 egg whites
1/4 tsp salt

**Garnish: whipped cream**

Melt butter in the top of a double boiler and stir in flour. Slowly stir in cream and coffee. Cook until sauce thickens.

Combine egg yolks and sugar. Add 2 or 3 Tbsp of the hot sauce to the egg yolks and stir eggs back into sauce. Remove from fire and stir until custard cools. Stir in almonds and vanilla.

Combine salt and egg whites and whip whites until stiff. Fold egg whites into coffee-almond custard and pour into a buttered 1 1/2 qt souffle dish.

Bake in a preheated 375 degree oven for 30 to 35 minutes. Garnish with whipped cream.

3 Tbsp butter
3 Tbsp flour
1 cup heavy cream
1/2 cup sugar
Juice of 2 lemons
2 lemon rinds, grated
4 egg yolks
6 egg whites

Melt butter in the top of a double boiler and add flour. Stir in cream and cook until sauce thickens. Gradually add sugar, lemon juice and lemon rinds.

Stir 2 or 3 Tbsp of lemon sauce into egg yolks and stir eggs back into sauce. Remove from fire and beat custard until cool.

Whip egg whites until stiff and fold into custard. Pour into a buttered 1 1/2 qt souffle dish. Bake in a pre-heated 375 degree oven for 30 to 35 minutes. Serve with the following Strawberry Sauce:

1 pint fresh strawberries,
  hulled and crushed
2 Tbsp red current jelly,
  whipped with fork.
2 Tbsp sugar
2 Tbsp Kirsch

Combine strawberries, jelly, sugar and Kirsch; and chill in the refrigerator for 4 hours.

3 Tbsp butter
3 Tbsp flour
3/4 cup milk
3 egg yolks, beaten
1/4 cup sugar
1 1/2 tsp vanilla
1/2 cup *creme de marrons glaces*
  (pureed chestnuts)
3 egg whites
1/4 tsp salt
1 Tbsp powdered sugar
1/2 cup heavy cream, whipped
1 Tbsp sugar
1/2 tsp vanilla

Melt butter in the top of a double boiler and add flour. Stir in milk and cook until sauce is quite thick.

Beat egg yolks with sugar and vanilla. Stir 2 or 3 Tbsp of hot sauce into egg yolks and stir eggs back into sauce. Remove from fire and add *creme de marron glaces* and blend well.

Combine salt with egg whites and whip whites until stiff. Fold egg whites into marron custard and pour into a buttered 1 qt souffle dish which has been sprinkled in the bottom with powdered sugar.

Place dish in a pan of hot water and bake in a preheated 325 degree oven for 1 1/2 hours. (This low-temperature baking insures a firmer center—which is preferable for this souffle.)

Serve with whipped cream sweetened with sugar and vanilla.

# Index 94